Badges of the International Christian Endeavor and World Christian Endeavor Conventions

By

Robert Danielson

Badges of the International Christian Endeavor and World Christian Endeavor conventions by Robert Danielson

First Fruits Press, ©2016
Digital version at http://place.asburyseminary.edu/christianendeavorbooks/43/

ISBN: 9781621715160 (print), 9781621715146 (digital), 9781621715153 (kindle)

First Fruits Press is a digital imprint of the Asbury Theological Seminary, B.L. Fisher Library. Asbury Theological Seminary is the legal owner of the material previously published by the Pentecostal Publishing Co. and reserves the right to release new editions of this material as well as new material produced by Asbury Theological Seminary. Its publications are available for noncommercial and educational uses, such as research, teaching and private study. First Fruits Press has licensed the digital version of this work under the Creative Commons Attribution Noncommercial 3.0 United States License. To view a copy of this license, visit http://creativecommons.org/licenses/by-nc/3.0/us/.

For all other uses, contact:

First Fruits Press
B.L. Fisher Library
Asbury Theological Seminary
204 N. Lexington Ave.
Wilmore, KY 40390
http://place.asburyseminary.edu/firstfruits

Danielson, Robert A. (Robert Alden), 1969-
  Badges of the International Christian Endeavor and World Christian Endeavor conventions / by Robert Danielson. -- Wilmore, Kentucky : First Fruits Press, ©2016.
    130 pages : color illustrations ; 21 cm.
    ISBN - 13: 9781621715160 (pbk.)
    1. International Society of Christian Endeavor--Medals, badges, decorations, etc. 2. United Society of Christian Endeavor--Medals, badges, decorations, etc. 3. World's Christian Endeavor Union--Medals, badges, decorations, etc. 4. Badges--Catalogs and collections. 5. Medals--Catalogs and collections. I. Title.
BV1421.D36 2016

Cover design by Jon Ramsay

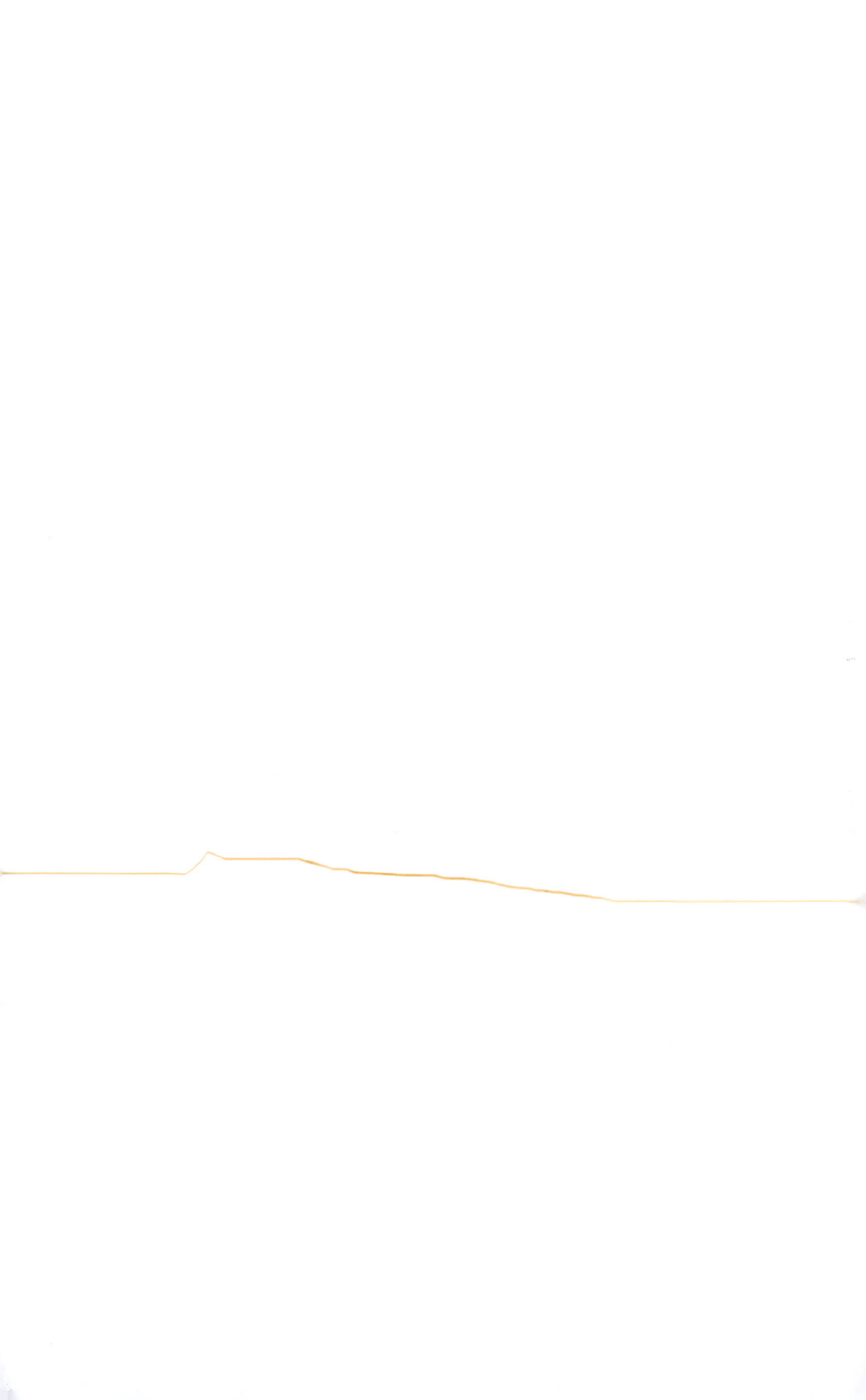

Badges of the International Christian Endeavor and World Endeavor Conventions

Table of Contents

Brief History of Christian Endeavor 1

Role of Badges in Christian Endeavor 5

List of International Conventions of Christian Endeavor 21

List of World Conventions of Christian Endeavor 25

Types of Badges and Dating 29

    Local, State and international C.E. Badges 32

    Buttons (With and Without Ribbons) 37

    Pins 40

    Nametags 41

    Other Types 42

Illustrations of Major Conventions in the Asbury Collection 45

Badges of the Annual Conference of the Y.P.S.C.E. and the International Conventions of Christian Endeavor (1882 - 1993) 51

Badges of the Annual Conference of the World Conventions of Christian Endeavor (1896 - 1990) 103

Brief History of Christian Endeavor

The Young People's Society of Christian Endeavor was formed in Portland, Maine at Williston Congregational Church on February 2, 1881. It began as a small effort by the pastor, Rev. Francis E. Clark to involve more young people in his congregation. At this time, there existed Sunday Schools for young children and regular Bible Studies and worship services for adults, but nothing was in place for young people who did not fall neatly into either category. As a result, many young people were leaving the church.

Rev. Clark formed this first Christian Endeavor Society in the parlor of the parsonage, where young people signed a pledge to be active participants "for Christ and the Church." They formed and ran their own committees and everyone was required to be involved in their worship activities beyond simply singing hymns. By giving the youth more responsibility and empowering them to live Christian lives in their society, the modern Youth Ministry Movement was born.

Christian Endeavor, as the Young People's Society of Christian Endeavor, soon became called, was the first Christian youth fellowship and became the forerunner for modern day youth ministry. Rev. Francis E. Clark became recognized as the "Father of Youth Ministry." The society grew rapidly and soon spread to all of the states of the United States and many other countries as well. It remained interdenominational, was interracial, and worked to include youth from all of the Protestant denominations.

While it faded over time, in its heyday it was a huge political and social force in the United States. Religious leaders of many denominations, as well as political leaders, including presidents of the United States, attended its annual and then biannual conventions. In the period following World War One, its numbers began to decline, in part as denominations founded their own youth fellowships in competition. Both the International Christian Endeavor organization (now called Endeavor: http://endeavormovement.com/) and the World Christian Endeavor organization still exist and operate their ministries, but they will forever leave their historical footprint in the realm of youth ministry.

Role of Badges in Christian Endeavor

Some of the memorabilia of Christian Endeavor in the history of Protestant Christianity includes the tremendous number of pins, ribbons, medals, banners, and other items left behind from this extensive movement. Being publically identified with the Christian Endeavor Movement was an important part of the experience, and these items can still be commonly found in various forms.

Badges (items specifically designed to be worn with the Christian Endeavor logo), either ribbons, pins, or a mixture of both, were a common feature of Christian Endeavor. In general, they served multiple purposes. First, they helped create and solidify a sense of identity within the group. Second, they were used as rewards and incentives to promote the growth of this youth ministry. Third, they sometimes served the practical function of entry tickets for large conventions. Fourth, they helped promote the ideals of Christian Endeavor to the wider community as a form of mission. Fifth, these badges were also used as a form of competition between various state and local societies, especially with the goal of expanding the outreach of Christian Endeavor.

There are no badges from the first three International Conventions (Portland, Maine 1882, Portland, Maine 1883, and Lowell, Massachusetts, 1884). The first mention of a badge is a ribbon used at the fourth International Convention in Old Orchard, Maine. The conference report notes,

> Announcement was made by the chair that badges had been prepared for the delegates, who were requested to provide themselves with the same that they might be distinguished from others in attendance, not delegates. The badges consisted of a piece of white satin ribbon, with the legend "Christian Endeavor, Delegate," printed thereon in red letters. Similar badges were provided for visitors.[1]

By the ninth International Convention, the number of visitors became rather unwieldy and the convention report notes, "Admission was gained

---

1   *Fourth Annual Conference of the Young People's Societies of Christian Endeavor Convention, 1885*, page 6.

on presentation of the convention badge."[2] This indicates that badges were not just used to separate delegates from visitors, but also to allow admission to particularly important events during the convention itself.

In identifying early badges and ribbons, it is important to note that the common logo of the "E" encased by the "C" was not adopted until November of 1887 (after the sixth annual conference in 1887). Ribbons from before 1888 are most likely to bear the initials "Y.P.S.C.E." for "The Young People's Societies of Christian Endeavor." It is unlikely that any pins, buttons, or medal-type badges were created before 1892, so most of the early badges will be ribbons. Items simply bearing the "Y.P.S.C.E." without the logo can be dated between 1885-1888. It is still common to see the "Y.P.S.C.E." logo on badges along with the C.E. logo as well, even after 1888.

Critical to the development of Christian Endeavor identity was the development of its primary logo, a "C" surrounding an "E." This logo was developed by Rev. Howard B. Grose in 1887, and has been defined as, "The C. embraces the E. The Endeavor is all within the Christ..."[3] Material from the early history of Christian Endeavor notes, "After the United Society was organized, one of the early matters pressing for action was the adoption of an official pin, in order to prevent the multiplication of styles otherwise inevitable."[4] The leaders of the Society patented the logo to prevent profiteers from making money on the society.

---

2   *Minutes of the Ninth Annual International Christian Endeavor Convention, Boston, MA*: The United Society of Christian Endeavor, 1890:5.
3   From Chapter 33, "Badges and Banners" in *World Wide Endeavor*, by Francis E. Clark, Philadelphia, PA: Gillespie and Metzgar, 1895:248.
4   Ibid.

Copy of Notes for the Christian Endeavor Logo Designed by Rev. Howard B. Grose in 1887[5]

After the early introduction of ribbons, local and state branches of Christian Endeavor began to produce their own versions for local and state conventions in their own local colors and a huge variety of designs. Because of this tremendous amount of variety, it is impossible to cover all possible types and derivations in this one book. For our purposes we will focus on the International Christian Endeavor conventions held in the United States and Canada, and the World Christian Endeavor conventions, which developed out of them.

Beyond badges for conventions, Christian Endeavor material included all kinds of pins, tie clasps, rings, bracelets, sweater clasps, banners, flags, and apparel of all kinds. This was true not just in the United States, but in various parts of the world as well. Most of this material is not dated, but it is usually clearly identified by the C.E. logo. Members desired to be recognized as part of the organization.

---

5   From Chapter 33, "Badges and Banners" in *World Wide Endeavor*, by Francis E. Clark, Philadelphia, PA: Gillespie and Metzgar, 1895:249. Image in the Public Domain.

"It is the custom of our society to give each new member a Christian Endeavor pin, in the hope that it will serve as an earnest (token?) of our brotherly affection, and as a constant reminder of the covenant you have just repeated with us. We ask that you show your Christian endeavor colors faithfully, and we pray that this little emblem may come to mean as much in your lives as it means in ours."[6]

One Christian Endeavor manual notes how some of this material was used,

"Celluloid buttons are cheap and they can be used as rewards for Junior work well done. When a Junior has earned so many buttons, he may exchange them for a Christian Endeavor pin. Every Junior should be encouraged to wear the Christian Endeavor monogram in some form or other, on a button or a pin. Make this a point of some of the contests the society carries out."[7]

Identification with the Society was important, but so was spiritual growth, and so buttons and pins were frequently used as ways to display membership, but also given as incentives for scripture memorization and other rewards.

---

6   Suggested wording for the reception of active members from *The Christian Endeavor Manual*, by Francis E. Clark, new and revised edition, Boston, MA: United society of Christian Endeavor, 1912:267.

7   *The New Junior Workers' Manual: A Textbook on Junior Work* by Rev. Robert P. Anderson. Boston, MA: United Society of Christian Endeavor 1921:180.

A Photograph of a Floating Christian Endeavorer, Elitson from the *USS Olympia*. Notice the C and E pin above the Dewey medal in this image. The Dewey medal was given to those who fought in the battle of Manila Bay in the Spanish-American War, and the *Olympia* was Dewey's flagship. Members of the Floating Christian Endeavor were permitted to wear their Christian Endeavor pins on their uniforms.

Drawing of Christian Endeavor Badges from Foreign Countries[8]

A final use of badges, especially ribbons, came in the creation of badge banners, which were made up of many donated ribbons sewn together. This was apparently first done at the ninth International Convention, and a reference from the following year notes,

> "At St. Louis, last year, a badge banner, made up, as it was, of badges from hundreds of societies, was displayed amidst much enthusiasm. Acting upon the suggestions made by a delegate, it was decided to place that banner for one year in the custody of the State, Territory, or Province that should show the greatest proportionate increase in its number of local societies during the year just closing."[9]

For a number of years these banners seem to have been awarded at the convention and these highly prized banners moved to various parts of the country and the world in a sort of friendly competition. Sadly, none of these badge banners are currently known to exist. By the 1905 convention, it appears that the badge banners were replaced by other banners to be given the various state unions based on the percentage of increases in their various unions.

---

    8   Drawing taken from "Two Decades of Christian Endeavor," by Amos R. Wells. *The American Monthly Review of Reviews*, 23(2):185-190, February 1901. This image is in the public domain and came from page 190 of the article.

    9   Narrative of the Tenth International Christian Endeavor Convention, Boston, MA: United society of Christian Endeavor, 1891:20.

Image of a Badge Banner (in lower left corner) Given to the Oklahoma Society in 1891 for the State, Province, or Territory with the Largest Relative Gain[10]

Four badge banners were given out by 1898. The winner would hold the banner till the following year's convention, when it would be passed on the to next winning group. The earliest badge banners were given for the greatest proportional increase in societies in a union and for the greatest total number of new societies in a union. In 1892, a third badge banner was introduced for the greatest number of new societies in a junior endeavor union, and in 1898 for the greatest proportional increase in societies in a junior endeavor union.

---

10 Photograph from *World Wide Endeavor: The Story of the Young People's Society of Christian Endeavor*, by Rev. Francis E. Clark. Philadelphia, PA: Gillespie and Metzgar 1895, page 255. This particular banner was given to Oklahoma in 1891, and then went to Manitoba, Canada in 1892, New Mexico in 1893, and West Virginia in 1894. Its current location is unknown. In fact, there are no known C.E. badge banners currently in existence.

Winners of the badge banner for the greatest proportional increase over the previous year for regular Christian Endeavor unions were:

Oklahoma	1891
Manitoba, Canada	1892
New Mexico	1893
West Virginia	1894
Assiniboia, Canada[11]	1895
Scotland	1896
Ireland	1897
South Africa	1898

Winners of the badge banner for the greatest total number of societies over the previous year for regular Christian Endeavor unions were:

Pennsylvania	1891
Ontario, Canada	1892
Pennsylvania	1893
England	1894
England	1895
England	1896
England	1897
Pennsylvania	1898

Winners of the badge banner for the greatest total number of societies over the previous year for Junior Christian Endeavor unions were:

Illinois	1892
New York	1893
Pennsylvania	1894
Pennsylvania	1895
Pennsylvania	1896
Ohio	1897
Pennsylvania	1898

---

11 Assiniboia was a district in Northwest Canada from the late 1800s until 1905 when it was absorbed mostly by Saskatchewan and to a lesser degree by Alberta.

Winners of the badge banner for the greatest proportional increase over the previous year for Junior Christian Endeavor unions were:

Washington, D.C.	1893
Delaware	1894
Assiniboia, Canada	1895
Mexico	1896
Spain	1897
India	1898

As badge banners came into short supply, leaders of the conventions took to offering banners, which had been sent by international groups of Christian Endeavors as prizes. Many of these banners are described in early convention reports, but sadly few exist today. Many of these banners came from China and Japan and were heavily embroidered. Some banners that were apparently not given as prizes still remain in the Christian Endeavor collection at Asbury Theological Seminary. Their ornate design and craftsmanship speak to the skill used in banner making at this time.

Role of Badges in Christian Endeavor | 15

An Embroidered Silk Chinese Banner dated 1905

Another Early Silk Chinese Banner

A Photograph of an Embroidered CE Banner for the Floating Societies of the Christian Endeavor dated 1895

Given the space limitations of this book, we will attempt to illustrate the major Christian Endeavor badges and their forms as used for the International and World Christian Endeavor Conventions, from their earliest days until 1993, which was the end of the International Christian Endeavor Conventions, and until 1990 for the World Christian Endeavor Conventions, which continue to be held. There are gaps in the collection for some of the earliest badges and some of the latest due to preservation issues. More recent badges were simply paper nametags, while the oldest badges were rare and fragile ribbons.

List of International Conventions of Christian Endeavor
(1882 - 1993)

1st	Portland, ME	1882
2nd	Portland, ME	June 7, 1883
3rd	Lowell, MA	Oct.23-24, 1884
4th	Old Orchard, ME	July 8-9, 1885
5th	Saratoga Springs, NY	July 6-8, 1886
6th	Saratoga Springs, NY	July 5-7, 1887
7th	Chicago, IL	July 5-8, 1888
8th	Philadelphia, PA	July 9-11, 1889
9th	St. Louis, MO	June 12-15, 1890
10th	Minneapolis/St. Paul, MN	July 9 - 12, 1891
	Portland, ME (Decennial convention)	Feb. 2-4, 1891
11th	New York, NY	July 7-10, 1892
12th	Montreal, Canada	July 5-9, 1893
13th	Cleveland, OH	July 11-15, 1894
14th	Boston, MA	July 10-15, 1895
15th	Washington, DC	July 8-13, 1896
16th	San Francisco, CA	July 7-12, 1897
17th	Nashville, TN	July 6-11, 1898
18th	Detroit, MI	July 5-10, 1899
19th	London, England	July 13-20, 1900
20th	Cincinnati, OH	July 6-10, 1901
21st	Denver, CO	July 9-13, 1903
22nd	Baltimore, MD	July 5-10, 1905
23rd	Seattle, WA	July 10-15, 1907
24th	St. Paul, MN	July 7-12, 1909
25th	Atlantic City, NJ	July 6-12, 1911
26th	Los Angeles, CA	July 9-14, 1913
27th	Chicago, IL	July 7-12, 1915
28th	New York, NY (Postponed until the end of World War I) Buffalo, New York (special convention)	July 4-9, 1917 Aug. 5-10, 1919
28th	New York, NY	July 6-13, 1921
29th	Des Moines, IA	July 4-9, 1923
30th	Portland, OR	July 4-10, 1925
31st	Cleveland, OH	July 2-7, 1927

32nd	Kansas City, MO	July 3-8, 1929
33rd	San Francisco, CA	July 11-16, 1931
34th	Milwaukee, WI	July 8-13, 1933
35th	Philadelphia, PA	July 2-7, 1935
36th	Grand Rapids, MI	July 8-13, 1937
37th	Cleveland, OH	July 6-11, 1939
38th	Atlantic City, NJ Estes Park, CO (Wartime convention)	July 8-13, 1941 July 6-11, 1943
39th	San Francisco, CA	July 8-13, 1947
40th	Toronto, Canada	July 5-10, 1949
41st	Grand Rapids, MI	July 9-15, 1951
42nd	Denver, CO	June 22-27, 1953
43rd	Columbus, OH	July 11-16, 1955
44th	Portland, OR	July 8-13, 1957
45th	Philadelphia, PA	July 6-11, 1959
46th	Chicago, IL	July 5-8, 1961
47th	Washington D.C.	July 2-6, 1963
48th	Dallas, TX	July 6-10, 1965
49th	Detroit, MI	July 3-7, 1967
50th	Kitchner-Waterloo, Canada	Aug. 19-23, 1970
51st	St. Louis, MO	July 5-9, 1971
52nd	Evansville, IN	July 2-6, 1973
53rd	Portland, OR	July 3-7, 1975
54th	Reading, PA	July 11-15, 1977
55th	Honolulu, HA	1979
56th	Portland, ME	Aug. 12-16, 1981
57th	Seattle, WA	July 4-8, 1983
58th	Holland, MI	July 1-5, 1985
59th	Buffalo, NY	July 6-10, 1987
60th	Harlingen, TX	July 3-7, 1989
61st	Annville, PA	July 1-5, 1991
62nd	Kailuna-Kona, HA	July 6-10, 1993

Christian Endeavor International Conventions ceased in 1993.

List of World Conventions of Christian Endeavor (1896 - 2018)

1st	Washington, DC	July 8-13, 1896 (15th International)
2nd	London, England	July 13-20, 1900 (19th International)
3rd	Geneva, Switzerland	July 28- Aug. 1, 1906
4th	Agra, India	Nov. 20-25, 1909
5th	Chicago, IL	July 7-12, 1915 (27th International)
6th	New York, NY	July 6-11, 1921 (28th International)
7th	London, England	July 16-21, 1926
8th	Berlin, Germany	Aug. 5-10, 1930
9th	Budapest, Hungary	Aug. 2-8, 1935 (originally for 1934)
10th	Melbourne, Australia	Aug. 2-8, 1938

(No Conventions Held During World War II)

11th	London, England	July 21-27, 1950
12th	Washington, D.C.	July 24-28, 1954
13th	Frankfurt, Germany	July 23-27, 1958
14th	Sydney, Australia	Aug. 16-21, 1962
15th	Belfast, Ireland	July 27-Aug. 1, 1966
16th	Kitchner-Waterloo, Canad	Aug. 19-23, 1970 (50th International)
17th	Essen, Germany	July 24-28, 1974
18th	New Delhi, India	Oct. 9-12, 1978
19th	Portland, ME	Aug. 12-16, 1981 (56th International)
20th	Seoul, Korea	Aug. 6-9, 1986
21st	Coventry, UK	July 31- Aug. 4, 1990
22nd	Merida, Mexico	Aug. 10-14, 1994
23rd	Bad Liebenzell, Germany	July 30- Aug. 2, 1998
24th	Singapore	June 1-6, 2002
25th	Gödöllő, Hungary	July 13-16, 2006
26th	Lima, Peru	Aug. 3-7, 2010
27th	Gangwon-do, Korea	July 23-26, 2014
28th	National City, CA	July 25-29, 2018

Types of Badges and Dating

As mentioned earlier, there is no evidence of any ribbons or badges used prior to 1885, when the first ribbon was used at the fourth International Christian Endeavor Convention to distinguish delegates from visitors. Items dating from 1885-1888 are likely to be identified from the letters "Y.P.S.C.E." and will not contain the C and E logo. After 1888 the "Y.P.S.C.E." can be found with the C and E logo, but over time this gives way to the use of "Christian Endeavor" with the C and E logo by the late 1890's and the early 1900's.

In terms of the International Christian Endeavor Conventions, simple ribbons were the first type of badges used, often printed with the date and place of the convention, and often the common slogan, "For Christ and the Church." This type of badge is found especially from 1885-1891. With a low cost, this form continued to be popular in local and state conventions for a number of years. These early ribbons are quite rare, since fewer were made and the material they are made from is not the best for good preservation.

From 1892-1921 was the high-water point of Christian Endeavor, and the badges used at the International Christian Endeavor Conventions became quite elaborate. Most follow a type similar to a military medal, with a bar pin and ribbon attached to a larger metal object suspended on the ribbon. This time period also coincides with the Spanish-American War and World War I. With their focus on youth ministry, and some of their special work with sailors (through the Floating Societies of Christian Endeavor) and the military, such a parallel with military medals should not be surprising. The imperialistic aims of the United States encouraged strong patriotism, and the parallels with the Christian Endeavor army moving across the globe on a mission for Christ, are clear to see.

With the end of the World War and the coming of the Great Depression, as well as the gradual decline in numbers, 1923-1937 enters a transitional phase for International Christian Endeavor badges. Cheaper versions of the military medal style were made using celluloid, thin plastic, or even paper. Ribbons continue to appear and inexpensive buttons also make a showing. Also individual nametags appear, although the frames for the individual's name are usually made of metal and are fairly ornate.

From 1939-1993, the individual nametag takes priority over the more group-oriented badges. The function of the badges moves from group identity to a practical approach to learning and remembering people's individual names. The ornate metal frames give way to simple paper nametags in simple plastic sleeves. Occasional special plastic badges were made for historic events, such as the fiftieth International Christian Endeavor Convention in 1970 and the 100th anniversary of Christian Endeavor in 1981.

The World Christian Endeavor Conventions were almost all represented by enameled pins to commemorate each convention. There is less variety of style over their years, and most of the pins clearly state the location and date of the convention.

Local, State, and International C.E. Badges

It is important to remember for those collecting or identifying Christian Endeavor material, that there are numerous examples of badges from local, state, and even other international conventions, and they can represent a wide range of types. While this book cannot hope to cover all, or even most, of the material that might still be found in collections, we will attempt to illustrate some of the potential types of badges that may be found.

Christian Endeavor was a truly international organization, and national conventions were held in a number of nations in the world. Some of these adopted the practice of using ribbons or badges within their own national organizations.

Woven Ribbon Badge from the 7th National Convention of the Christian Endeavor Union of Great Britain and Ireland held in Liverpool, England in 1897

Within the various local and state conventions, ribbons seem to be the most popular types of badges to be used. Sometimes these are simple ribbons held on by a straight pin, but sometimes they were more elaborate with a bar pin at the top (sometimes ornate and sometimes plain) and decorated with various local images.

Two State Convention Ribbons, one without a bar pin at the top (from Maine, Sept. 4-6, 1908) and one with a bar pin at the top (from Pennsylvania, Aug. 22-25, 1895)

Occasionally more elaborate military-type medal pins were used for local and state conventions. Some of these would have metal objects attached at the end of the ribbon and others would use celluloid, Bakelite, or other material. Most of these do have an elaborate pin bar at the top of the badge.

Badge for the 22nd Annual California Union Convention held in Pasadena, CA in 1909.

Two Medal-Type Badges with an ornate pin bar, ribbon, and suspended element, in these cases made of celluloid. The first is actually for the 25th International C.E. Convention, but this is a badge made specifically for the Indiana delegation to Atlantic City, N.J. (July 6-12, 1911). The second example is from the Kentucky State Convention (Louisville, May 13-15, 1910).

Buttons (with and without ribbons)

As Christian Endeavor ephemera became more popular within the organization, various metal buttons were used, sometimes with ribbons highlighting special conventions, but also simply for use and collection by enthusiastic members.

Examples of general buttons used with ribbons for local events.

Both of these examples are from the Annual Kansas State Convention, at Hutchinson, KS June 11 - 13, 1912 (on the left) and Kansas City, KS June 20 - 22, 1911 (on the right).

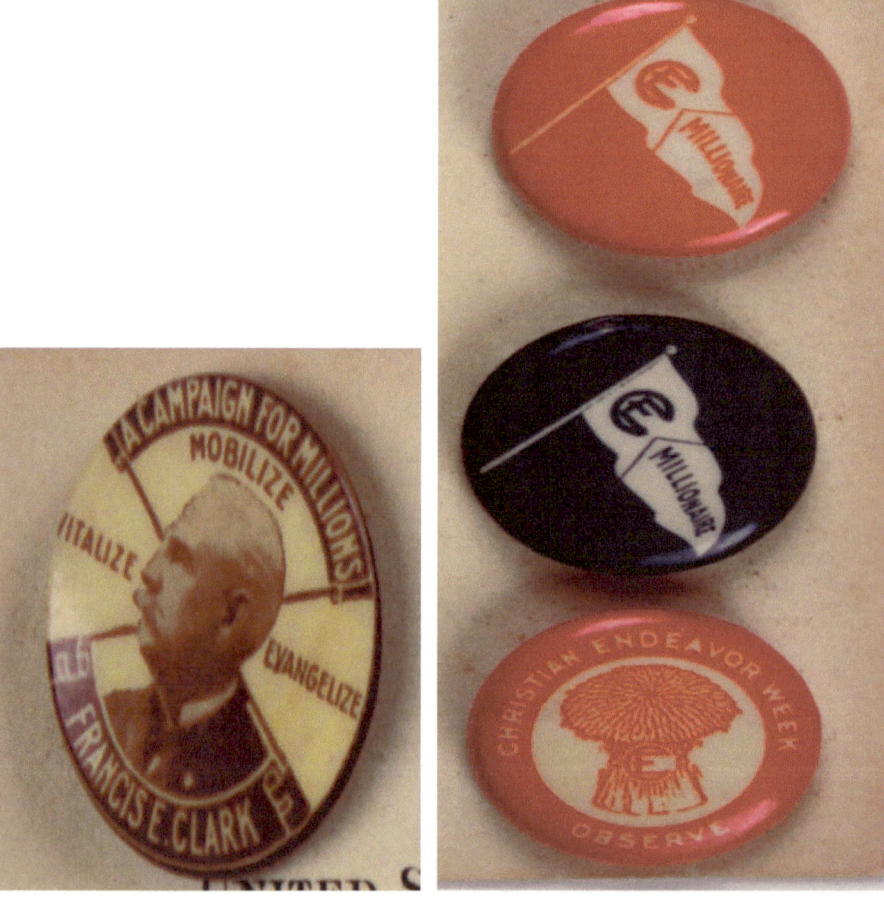

Examples of buttons made for specific campaigns.

Examples of buttons used for major conventions although not used as official badges.

Pins

While occasional pins are found for Christian Endeavor in general, their use for major conventions was mostly limited to World Conventions. These pins are usually more elaborate than the more frequent buttons, and often enameled.

This pin is most likely the official pin from the 8th World's Convention held in Berlin in 1930.

Nametags

Nametags became popular options during periods of economic scarcity and later came into use in the history of Christian Endeavor as the group identity focus of the badges began to decline.

This unusual paper nametag used during World War II is still shaped like its earlier medal-type precursors. It was used for a special one day convention during World War II in the Michigan State Christian Endeavor Union.

Other Types

Some types of badges used in Christian Endeavor defy categorizing. Ribbon, plastics, celluloid, metal, paper, and even yarn and plastic canvas could be used to create memorable badges for the society's many meetings and conventions at all levels: local, state, national, international, or world.

This plastic and ribbon badge from the 1901 Michigan State Convention in Port Huron (March 26 -28, 1901) is an unusual shape and style for a Christian Endeavor badge.

Illustrations of Major Conventions in the Asbury Collection

The International Christian Endeavor and World Christian Endeavor collections at Asbury Theological Seminary contain only a few examples of the early ribbons. These are very fragile and hard to find. Also, there were fewer delegates to these earlier conventions and so the numbers of badges produced makes them difficult to collect. The conference journals can give us a rough idea of how many people attended the conventions from their attendance estimates. This may give an idea of how many ribbons were produced in these early years.

In the Second Annual Conference held in Portland, Maine (1883), there were only 71 delegates. This rose to 137 for the Third Annual Conference in Lowell, Massachusetts (1884) and 161 delegates for the Fourth Annual Conference in Old Orchard, Maine (1885), where we have the first mention of a ribbon to be worn by delegates. By the Seventh Annual Conference in Chicago (1888), there were some 4,000 delegates. In the Ninth Annual Conference of the Y.P.S.C.E. (1890) (the last before the name changed to International Christian Endeavor Convention), there were 4,500 delegates gathered in St. Louis, Missouri.

By the next convention, the Tenth International Christian Endeavor Convention in Minneapolis, Minnesota (1891), there was a staggering 14,000 delegates and visitors gathered together! By the Eleventh International Convention in New York City (1892), there were 32,000 delegates registered, and by the Fourteenth International Convention in Boston in 1895, there were over 56,000 people in attendance. This is often viewed as the largest Christian Endeavor Conference held duirng its history.

At the Boston Convention of 1895, the global growth of the Christian Endeavor Movement was recognized by the formation of the World Christian Endeavor, which would begin taking on more of the focus on work outside of the United States and Canada. For a short time the International Christian Endeavor Convention was held jointly with the World Christian Endeavor Convention, especially with the turmoil of World War I in Europe. But even with this situation, the Sixteenth International Convention in San Francisco, California (1897) recorded between 25,000 and 30,000 delegates.

The Nineteenth International Convention was also the Second World Christian Endeavor Convention and was held with great fanfare in London, England in 1900. While the exact number of people in attendance is unknown, delegates and visitors filled Royal Albert Hall and Alexandra Palace. Global representatives brought greetings during the waning years of Queen Victoria, who even made a special appearance to a group of Christian Endeaver who came to pay their respects. This was the only International Convention held outside of the United States or Canada.

After the 1901 convention in Cincinnati, Ohio, the International Christian Endeavor Conventions moved from being an annual event to being held every other year. The World Christian Endeavor Conventions were held roughly every four years. Except for short postponements during the World Wars, both conventions stayed close to this schedule. However, attendance at these conventions had peaked and began to decline at this time.

Christian Endeavor by this time had established a strong political influence in the US. While the opening session of the Twenty-fifth International Convention in Atlantic City, New Jersey (1911) held over 6,000 people, this convention would become well-known for the presence and speeches of the president of the United States, William Taft. Other presidents would attend before their time in office (President McKinley spoke while he was the governor of Ohio at the Cleveland Convention in 1894), and others would speak after their time in office (former President Herbert Hoover spoke in the Cleveland Convention of 1939), and many would send letters, telegraphed greetings, and even a live radio address (also by President Hoover at the 1931 San Francisco Convention). Christian Endeavor saw itself as a force for advocating prohibition, but also advocating good citizenship and creating a sense of civic responsibility in the youth of its day.

Because of all these factors, it is difficult to assign any convention the title of "high water mark" of the Christian Endeavor movement. The Boston Convention of 1895 with over 56,000 in attendance, the global London Convention of 1900, or the political power of President Taft's presence in the 1911 Atlantic City Convention, all offer good possibilities. Nevertheless, while numbers began to decline sometime after this period, Christian Endeavor remained a global force and continued to influence thousands of the youth of America for many years to come. It continues today with both the Endeavor Movement headquartered in Edmore, Michigan and the World Christian Endeavor headquartered in Germany. The history of this movement, and the badges that represent it present a fascinating look at material Christianity in the late 19th and early 20th century, and how it harnessed the power and enthusiasm of its youth.

Badges of the Annual Conference of the Y.P.S.C.E. and the International Conventions of Christian Endeavor (1882- 1993)

1st Annual Conference of the Y.P.S.C.E
Portland, ME
1882
No known badge.

2nd Annual Conference of the Y.P.S.C.E
Portland, ME
June 7, 1883
No known badge.
For details on this convention see:
http://place.asburyseminary.edu/ceinternationalbooks/1/

3rd Annual Conference of the Y.P.S.C.E
Lowell, MA
Oct. 23-24, 1884
No known badge.
For details on this convention see:
http://place.asburyseminary.edu/ceinternationalbooks/17/

4th Annual Conference of the Y.P.S.C.E
Old Orchard, ME
July 8-9, 1885

First mention of a badge (none in this collection). Described as a white satin ribbon with red letters saying "Christian Endeavor, Delegate."

For details on this convention see:

http://place.asburyseminary.edu/ceinternationalbooks/2/

5th Annual Conference of the Y.P.S.C.E
Saratoga, NY
July 6-8, 1886

No badge in this collection.
For details on this convention see:
http://place.asburyseminary.edu/ceinternationalbooks/37/

6th Annual Conference of the Y.P.S.C.E
Saratoga, NY
July 5-7, 1887

No badge in this collection.

For details on this convention see:
http://place.asburyseminary.edu/ceinternationalbooks/36/

7th Annual Conference of the Y.P.S.C.E
Chicago, IL
July 5-8, 1888

No badge in this collection.
For details on this convention see:
http://place.asburyseminary.edu/ceinternationalbooks/25/

8th Annual Conference of the Y.P.S.C.E
Philadelphia, PA
July 9-11, 1889
For details on the convention see:
 http://place.asburyseminary.edu/ceinternationalbooks/12/

9th Annual Conference of the Y.P.S.C.E
St. Louis, MO
June 12-15, 1890
For details on the convention see:
http://place.asburyseminary.edu/ceinternationalbooks/14/

10th International Christian Endeavor Convention
Minneapolis/ St. Paul, MN
July 9-12, 1891

Here is both the delegate badge and the badge for general visitors for the same convention. As Christian Endeavor grew in popularity more visitors became common and it was difficult to tell them apart from voting delegates for the business meetings.
For details on the convention see:
http://place.asburyseminary.edu/ceinternationalbooks/26/

11th International Christian Endeavor Convention
New York, NY
July 7-10, 1892
The number of attendees was so large the supply of badges and programs were gone by the end of the first day, and frequently delegates had to be turned away from the venue in Madison Square Gardens.
For details on the convention see:
http://place.asburyseminary.edu/ceinternationalbooks/20/

12th International Christian Endeavor Convention
Montreal, Canada
July 5-9, 1893

13th International Christian Endeavor Convention
Cleveland, OH
July 11-15, 1894

For details on the convention see:
http://place.asburyseminary.edu/ceinternationalbooks/41/

14th International Christian Endeavor Convention
Boston, MA
July 10-15, 1895

For details on the convention see:
http://place.asburyseminary.edu/ceinternationalbooks/27/

**15th International Christian Endeavor Convention
1st World Convention of Christian Endeavor
Washington, DC
July 8-13, 1896.
For details on the convention see:**
http://place.asburyseminary.edu/ceinternationalbooks/15/

16th International Christian Endeavor Convention
San Francisco, CA
July 7-12, 1897
For details on the convention see:
http://place.asburyseminary.edu/ceinternationalbooks/21/

While there is no example of this badge in the Asbury Theological Seminary collection, this image of the front and back was provided courtesy of American Civil War Museum, Museum of the Confederacy Collection in Richmond, Virginia.

17th International Christian Endeavor Convention
Nashville, TN
July 6-11, 1898

For details on the convention see:
http://place.asburyseminary.edu/ceinternationalbooks/22/

18th International Christian Endeavor Convention
Detroit, MI
July 5-10, 1899

For details on the convention see:
http://place.asburyseminary.edu/ceinternationalbooks/24/

19th International Christian Endeavor Convention
2nd World Convention of Christian Endeavor
London, England
July 13-20, 1900

One of these badges is a celluloid version and the other is an enameled pin. Both were probably available at the convention for different price ranges.

For details on the convention see:
http://place.asburyseminary.edu/ceinternationalbooks/38/

20th International Christian Endeavor Convention
Cincinnati, OH
July 6-10, 1901

For details on the convention see:
http://place.asburyseminary.edu/ceinternationalbooks/33/

21st International Christian Endeavor Convention
Denver, CO
July 9-13, 1903

For details on the convention see:
http://place.asburyseminary.edu/ceinternationalbooks/40/

**22nd International Christian Endeavor Convention
Baltimore, MD
July 5-10, 1905**

For details on the convention see:
http://place.asburyseminary.edu/ceinternationalbooks/7/

**23rd International Christian Endeavor Convention
Seattle, WA
July 10-15, 1907**

For details on the convention see:
http://place.asburyseminary.edu/ceinternationalbooks/13/

24th International Christian Endeavor Convention
St. Paul, MN
July 7-12, 1909

For details on the convention see:
http://place.asburyseminary.edu/ceinternationalbooks/18/

25th International Christian Endeavor Convention
Atlantic City, NJ
July 6-12, 1911

For details on the convention see:
http://place.asburyseminary.edu/ceinternationalbooks/31/

26th International Christian Endeavor Convention
Los Angeles, CA
July 9-14, 1913

For details on the convention see:
http://place.asburyseminary.edu/ceinternationalbooks/30/

27ᵗʰ International Christian Endeavor Convention
5ᵗʰ World Convention of Christian Endeavor
Chicago, IL
July 7-12, 1915

For details on the convention see:
http://place.asburyseminary.edu/ceinternationalbooks/29/

28th International Christian Endeavor Convention
6th World Convention of Christian Endeavor
New York, NY
July 6-13, 1921

Note: This convention was originally scheduled for July 4-9, 1917, but was postponed until the end of World War I. However, the bar of the pin carries the 1917 date, while the added blue and white ribbon bears the 1921 date on which the convention was actually held.

For details on the convention see:
http://place.asburyseminary.edu/ceinternationalbooks/16/

29th International Christian Endeavor Convention
Des Moines, IA
July 4-9, 1923

For details on the convention see:
http://place.asburyseminary.edu/ceinternationalbooks/19/

30th International Christian Endeavor Convention
Portland, OR
July 4-10, 1925

For details on the convention see:
http://place.asburyseminary.edu/ceinternationalbooks/23/

31st International Christian Endeavor Convention
Cleveland, OH
July 2-7, 1927

For details on the convention see:
http://place.asburyseminary.edu/ceinternationalbooks/3/

32ⁿᵈ International Christian Endeavor Convention
Kansas City, MO
July 3-8, 1929

For details on the convention see:
http://place.asburyseminary.edu/ceinternationalbooks/9/

33rd International Christian Endeavor Convention
San Francisco, CA
July 11-16, 1931

For details on the convention see:
http://place.asburyseminary.edu/ceinternationalbooks/8/

34th International Christian Endeavor Convention
Milwaukee, WI
July 8-13, 1933

For details on the convention see:
http://place.asburyseminary.edu/ceinternationalbooks/10/

**35th International Christian Endeavor Convention
Philadelphia, PA
July 2-7, 1935**

**36th International Christian Endeavor Convention
Grand Rapids, MI
July 8-13, 1937**

For details on the convention see:
http://place.asburyseminary.edu/ceinternationalbooks/6/

37th International Christian Endeavor Convention
Cleveland, OH
July 6-11, 1939

For details on the convention see:
http://place.asburyseminary.edu/ceinternationalbooks/11/

38th International Christian Endeavor Convention
Atlantic City, NJ
July 8-13, 1941

For details on the convention see:
http://place.asburyseminary.edu/ceinternationalbooks/5/

39th International Christian Endeavor Convention
San Francisco, CA
July 8-13, 1947

40th International Christian Endeavor Convention
Toronto, Canada
July 5-10, 1949

41ˢᵗ International Christian Endeavor Convention
Grand Rapids, MI
July 9-15, 1951

For details on the convention see:
http://place.asburyseminary.edu/ceinternationalbooks/4/

43rd International Christian Endeavor Convention
Columbus, OH
July 11-16, 1955

45th International Christian Endeavor Convention
Philadelphia, PA
July 6-11, 1959

46th International Christian Endeavor Convention
CHICAGO, ILLINOIS   JULY 5-8, 1961

Elwood Dunn

Detroit, Michigan

 Venture With Christ

46th International Christian Endeavor Convention
Chicago, IL
July 5-8, 1961

48th International Christian Endeavor Convention
Dallas, TX
July 6-10, 1965

50th International Christian Endeavor Convention
16th World's Christian Endeavor Convention
Kitchner-Waterloo, Canada
Aug. 19-23, 1970

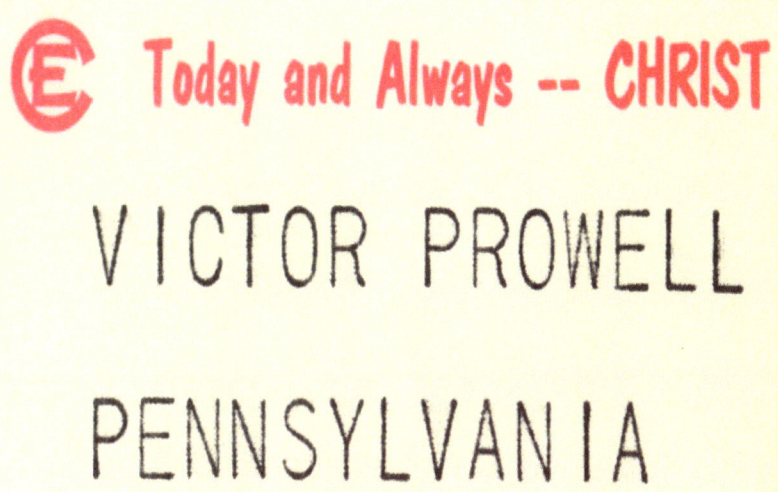

51st International Christian Endeavor Convention
St. Louis, MO
July 5-9, 1971

54th International Christian Endeavor Convention
Reading, PA
July 11-15, 1977

56th International Christian Endeavor Convention
19th World's Christian Endeavor Convention
Portland, Maine
Aug. 12-16, 1981

Held jointly in honor of the 100th year of Christian Endeavor's founding in Portland, Maine.

57th International Christian Endeavor Convention
Seattle, WA
July 4-8, 1983

58th International Christian Endeavor Convention
Holland, MI
July 1-5, 1985

60th International Christian Endeavor Convention
Harlingen, TX
July 3-7, 1989

61ˢᵗ International Christian Endeavor Convention
Annville, PA
July 1-5, 1991

62nd International Christian Endeavor Convention
Kona, HI
July 6-10, 1993

Badges of the World Conventions of Christian Endeavor
(1896 - 1990)

1ˢᵗ World Convention of Christian Endeavor
Washington, DC
July 8-13, 1896.

Held jointly with the 15ᵗʰ International Christian Endeavor Convention.

For details on the convention see:
http://place.asburyseminary.edu/ceinternationalbooks/15/

2nd World Convention of Christian Endeavor
London, England
July 13-20, 1900

Held jointly with the 19th International Christian Endeavor Convention.

One of these badges is a celluloid version and the other is an enameled pin. The two were probably both available in different price ranges.

For details on the convention see:
http://place.asburyseminary.edu/ceinternationalbooks/38/

5th World Convention of Christian Endeavor
Chicago, IL
July 7-12, 1915

Held jointly with the 27th International Christian Endeavor Convention.

For details on the convention see:
http://place.asburyseminary.edu/ceinternationalbooks/29/

6th World Convention of Christian Endeavor
New York, NY
July 6-13, 1921

Held jointly with the 28th International Christian Endeavor Convention.

Note: This convention was originally scheduled for July 4-9, 1917, but was postponed until the end of World War I. However, the bar of the pin carries the 1917 date, while the added blue and white ribbon bears the 1921 date on which the convention was actually held.

For details on the convention see:
http://place.asburyseminary.edu/ceinternationalbooks/16/

7th World's Christian Endeavor Convention
London, England
July 16-21, 1926

8th World's Christian Endeavor Convention
Berlin, Germany
Aug. 5-10, 1930

The first pin is possibly the official pin for this convention, although there is no date or information beyond the name of the city, Berlin. It is in keeping with the general design of the official badges of the World's Convention, which were usually enameled pins. The second badge is designed specifically for the U.S. delegation to the Berlin convention.

9th World's Christian Endeavor Convention
Budapest, Hungary
Aug. 2-8, 1935 (originally for 1934)

10th World's Christian Endeavor Convention
Melbourne, Australia
Aug. 2-8, 1938

11th World's Christian Endeavor Convention
London, England
July 21-27, 1950

12th World's Christian Endeavor Convention
Washington, DC
July 24-28, 1954

13th World's Christian Endeavor Convention
Frankfurt, Germany
July 23-27, 1958

14th World's Christian Endeavor Convention
Sydney, Australia
Aug. 16-21, 1962

15th World's Christian Endeavor Convention
Belfast, Ireland
July 27- Aug. 1, 1966

Badges of the World Conventions of Christian Endeavor | 117

**16th World's Christian Endeavor Convention
Kitchner-Waterloo, Canada
Aug. 19-23, 1970**

Held jointly in honor of the 50th year of the International Christian Endeavor Convention.

17th World's Christian Endeavor Convention
Essen, Germany
July 24-28, 1974

19th World's Christian Endeavor Convention
Portland, Maine
Aug. 12-16, 1981

Held jointly in honor of the 100th year of Christian Endeavor's founding in Portland, Maine, with the 56th International Christian Endeavor Convention.

20th World's Christian Endeavor Convention
Seoul, Korea
Aug. 6-9, 1986

21st World's Christian Endeavor Convention
Coventry, United Kingdom
July 31- Aug. 4, 1990

www.ingramcontent.com/pod-product-compliance
Lightning Source LLC
Chambersburg PA
CBHW042321150426
43192CB00001B/13